Random Facts and Trivia

Book 1

By Jack Lexington

Introduction

Hello and thank you for taking an interest in this book. This is the second fact book I Have produced the first being "The A-Z Of Random Facts". Even though that book was full of interesting bits of trivia, however I feel with experience and hindsight it could have been so much more. So I decided that for this book I would use a different set up. At some point I May even bring out a second edition of the "A-Z of Random Facts" written with this format.

The way this book will be set out is that not only will you get the fact but also an explanation for the fact that will take up 1-2 pages and will also contain little bonus facts related to the main fact.

I hope you enjoy the book and maybe learn something along the way.

<u>Fact 1</u>

King Charles II saved Christmas:

Yes I know what your thinking how did King Charles II save Christmas? Well I shall tell you, after the /English Civil War was over and Oliver Cromwell had achieved his victory, he put many unusual laws in place that affected many things, including making Christmas illegal. (Think the Sheriff of Nottingham's line in Robin Hood Prince of Thieves: "I'm cancelling Christmas!") King Charles II returned and won back the throne from Oliver Cromwell thus reinstating the Monarchy.

As King he threw out the laws making Christmas illegal and generally making England less uptight and more fun well apart from the Great fire of London Which King Charles actually played an active role in fighting risking his own life which just increased his popularity in Great Britain, There was also the second Anglo-Dutch wars during his reign Oh and a Plague in 1665. But surely Charles could not be blamed for that.

Fact 2

The USA had plans to attack Great Britain:

That's right two countries said to be "Closest allies" could have been broken up by the USA stabbing Great Britain in the back known as "Plan Red" which was drawn up in 1930

The USA had planned to attack with bombs and use chemical weapons to wipe out most of the British land forces in the North Atlantic attacking territories such as Canada thus cutting off Britain's trading points and essentially bringing the country to its knees. The USA used Charles Lindburgh to spy on areas that would offer the least resistance to set up bases along the Hudson Bay and actually did start to put their plan in to action by making manoeuvres. such as in 1935 placing troops and munition dumps at Fort Drum which was close to the Eastern Canadian border, which was where they planned to launch their initial attacks. With Halifax,Nova Scotia its target.

Churchill knew a war with the USA while not ideal was possible and Hitler believed a war between Britain and the USA was inevitable and hoped for a British victory.

but why?

Some speculate that the reason was that America seen itself as a rising power and a world leader during a time when Britain still had an expansive Empire. The USA had seen what Great Britain had done to upstarts who would try to upset the apple cart they would fight them and beat them. Were the USA just giving themselves a head-start should it come to that? Either way as a British Citizen I can only say I am glad that the plan did not come to fruition. In the end Franklin D Roosevelt deemed the plans to be inapplicable but should be kept aside which they were. Eventually America joined their close allies in a war against the Nazi regime and together the allied forces were victorious and the rest as they say is history.

Fact 3

The rats were not to blame for the spread of the Black Death:

For a long time a lot of people believed that rats and their fleas were the carriers of the Bubonic Plague, The Black death was not carried by the rats however but it is now deduced looking at the evidence,was passed person to person..The evidence for this also seems to suggest that the Black Death was not even the Bubonic Plague but an unknown disease. it seemed to escalate during the winter, however rats are not as active during the colder months, so this would suggest rats are not to blame, also there have never been many rat bones found from that time infected with the plague. Rats would have been infected by it to and if they were the carriers mass amounts of bones from plague infected rats should have been found at archaeological dig sites, furthering the claims it was a human to human spread disease.

Fact 4

We all live in the past:

That is right we are all living in the past......kind of. The reason is because after researching and documenting their findings a group of scientists have discovered that the human brain takes around 80 milliseconds to process the present so when you see something or hear something it happened around 80milliseconds beforehand.

I suppose it is similar to the fact that when we look in to space we are not seeing space at the present time but rather how it was a second or so ago. This is due to the time it takes light to travel from there to your eye. Or when you hear a plane, you look up sometimes you cant see it. That is because light travels faster than sound so you are essentially listening to the past and the plane may have moved on by that point, even if you do see a plane you are seeing how it was a fraction of a second earlier.

Fact 5

There are only 8 planets in our solar system:

If you are like me you grew up being told and having it drummed in to your head that there are nine planets in our solar system. Turns out this was not true there is only eight planets in our solar system they are Earth,Mars,Jupiter,Saturn,Neptune,Uranus, Venus and Mercury.

But wait what happened to Pluto? Well in recent times Pluto has been demoted to what is known as a Dwarf Planet there are a number of these in our solar system they are: Ceres Haumea, Makemake, Eris and now Pluto.

Fact 6

A Russian tsar held a court case to sentence a rat to death::

That is right Russia has had some crazy leaders in it's time and Tsar Peter III ranks right up there with them. Eventually dethroned due to his madness and hatred for his own country, He was replaced by Catherine the Great one of Russia's Greatest leaders.

Tsar Peter III had a collection of toy soldiers which he would play with and set up on a map, Unfortunately a rat liked to play with them to and chewed them. This infuriated Tsar Peter who set about catching the culprit. He succeeded and ordered the courts to hold a military trial for the rat which resulted in the rat being court marshalled for treason and sentenced to die by hanging.

Tsar Peter III built a tiny gallows and carried out the rats sentence. Hanging him he left the rats gallows there as a warning to other rats not to eat his toys.

Fact 7

We all have our own personal air conditioning system:

The human nose is our own personal heating and cooling system as one of it's functions is to cool the hot air we inhale and warm the cold air.

Other useful functions of the nose is it can help with balance and collecting moisture from the air as we are moving around.

The nose is also a factory for our sense of smell but sometimes foreign particles get in and irritate the nasal passage which is what in most cases causes us to sneeze.

Another cause of sneezing however much more rare is when your suddenly exposed to a bright light this is called a Photic sneeze reflex.

Fact 8

There is gold in your mobile phone:

This is factually correct inside a tonne weight of phones is about 300g of gold so if old phones were recycled it would take around 41 handsets to make the same amount of gold as it takes a tonne of ore to produce.

However phones are not the only surprising things that contain gold there is something a little more personal to you....your own body. That is right the human body contains particles of gold in areas such as the heart and your big toe nail of all places.

I wonder if you could take your toe nail clippings to a cash for gold company?.....probably not.

Fact 9

William Shakespeare invented the knock knock joke.:

That is right the great bard of Avon excellent storyteller and playwright created many things in terms of phrases and words including the knock knock joke which was first used in the second act of Macbeth in around 1606 it involves the heavily hungover porter inviting imaginary people in to his own personal hell.

Shakespeare as mentioned invented many sayings here are just a few of them some you may still hear being used today. We shall dedicate a couple of pages to his sayings:

"A wild goose chase"

"As good luck would have it"

"Bated breath"

"Neither a borrower nor a lender be"

"Be all and end all"

"Break the ice"

"Brevity is the soul of wit"

"Refuse to budge an inch"

"Dead as a doornail"

"Cry havoc and let slip the dogs of war"

"Devil incarnate"

"Eaten me out of house and home"

"Faint hearted"

"Fancy free"

"Forever and a day"

"For goodness sake"

"Foregone conclusion"

"Full circle"

"Give the devil his due"

"Good riddance"

"Jealousy the green eyed monster"

"Heart of gold"

"Hoist with his own petard"

"In my heart of hearts"

"In my minds eye"

"Kill with kindness"

"Laughing stock"

"live long day"

"Love is blind"

"Milk of human kindn2ess"

"One fell swoop"

"Play fast and loose"

and finally..."Wear my heart on my sleeve"

Fact 10

The first name recorded on a document or in writing of any kind was that of Kushim:

So who was Kushim? Was he a king? Or a high priest? Maybe a famous warrior or high standing citizen....the answer is none of the above Kushim was in fact an accountant. So how do we know his name? Well thanks to research carried out by Yuval Noah Kushim there has been discovered an engraved tablet dating back around 5,000 BC which appears to show a business deak bears the name Kushim this appears to be the oldest documented name written or engraved on any paper or tablet.

It is the ldest written name 30,000 years ago however writing had not been invented yet mankind still found a way to document the fact they existed through cave paintings and such. One technique was to leave their hand-print upon a rock-face some of which are still visible today.

<u>Fact 11</u>

**The biggest empire of all time is the
British empire::**

The British empire at it's peak is he biggest
that has ever existed containing an
estimated population of 533 million which
was around 20% of the worlds entire
population at the time.

The British empire was so vast that it
covered around 13 million square miles.
That accounts for around 22.63% of the
worlds total land mass.

The second largest of all time in terms of
land mass covered is the Mongolian empire
which covered 22.29% of the worlds land
mass. However this only accounted for a
population of around 110 million

Fact 12

Heroin was once advertised and marketed as a non addictive drug:

Between 1898 and 1910 Diamorphine was marketed under the name Heroin and was said to be a non addictive substitute for Morphine and used as a cough suppressant.

Diamorphine is still used in some hospitals today as a painkiller it was mainly used in the UK til around 2005 when there was a problem with supplies and hospitals switched to Morphine, even though there is no longer a supply or manufacturing problem many hospitals now stick with Morphine rather than going back to Diamotphine.

Fact 13

Actor Brad Pitt's first job involved him dancing in a chicken suit:

Before Brad Pitt made it big as an actor he had a job working for a company called El Pollo Loco which involved him dressing up as a giant chicken and trying to entice new customers in to the restaurant.

El Pollo Loco is a restaurant chain based in the USA it's speciality is Mexican style grilled chicken. It was founded in Guasave, Mexico in 1975 by Juan Francisco Ochoa.

Fact 14

The Indianapolis 500 track is 2.5 miles long:

The Indianapolis 500 which is held every year at the Indianapolis Motor speedway track. Is a race that consists of 200 laps around a 2.5mile long oval track to accumulate a distance of 500miles.

The race is usually held around the same time of year if not on the same day as The Memorial day holiday.

The race was first held in 1911 and there have been around 100 editions of the race at the time of writing this.

Fact 15

A Hippo provides it's own sunscreen:

A Hippo provides its own sunscreen through its sweat which is reddish in colour and the oily secretion is made up of two unstable pigments one is a red pigment the other is an orange pigment.

On the Hippos skin are pores that exude droplets of moisture containing the aforementioned red pigment, as light is reflected through the droplets they appear red which is where the statement that hippos sweat blood appears to come from..

A common misconception however is that the Hippo sweat is only red when it is angry or upset, this is not the case.

Fact 16

Snow White was originally called Snowdrop:

Disney's snow white was based on a story by the brothers Grimm in which the main character was called Snowdrop.

The Disney adaptation follows the same plot line as Snowdrop as do many of there Stories follow brothers Grimm such as Cinderella and Sleeping Beauty called Briar rose in the brothers Grimm version.

Jacob and Wilhelm Grimm collected and created many of the fairy-tales known and loved today.

Fact 17

Animals can dream:

Researchers have determined that the prior belief that very few species of animals dream is in fact false.

They now believe the majority of animals dream, they believe the core of these dreams that take place when animals sleep are like memories that are replayed in the head of the sleeping animal.

This was found by measuring and mapping the brain of rats who had been trained to run on a treadmill they measured the rats with electrodes as they were awake and running. And discovered like humans rats get REM (Rapid Eye Movement) while sleeping) and after comparing the rats data when awake to when they were asleep they found the brain activity supported there theory that animals dream.

Fact 18

The NFL makes an annual revenue of around $9billion:

The NFL makes around $13 billion per year making it one of if not the most successful sporting franchises in the world. This has been achieved through many factors including a strong negotiator getting them the best possible deal with regards to things such as sponsors and television rights..

Obviously vitally important is they have a shrewd businessman at the head of affairs who appears to know the game and its marketing value inside out. He has also stated that by the time 2027 comes he wants the NFL to be making around $25 billion per year. I for one see no reason why he cannot achieve this. In-fact in just 2-3yrs they have increased their annual take from around $9 billion in 2013 to $13 billion in 2015 so would not surprise me if they met that $25 billion target sooner than anticipated.

Fact 19

Fish breath oxygen through their gills.:

The gills of fish are feathery organs full of blood vessels. They are very important as when fish breath in water they force it out through their gills. As the water is forced out of the gills it scrapes across the gill walls which does its job in collecting dissolved oxygen from the water as it passes through.

The newly collected dissolved oxygen moves into the blood and travels to the fish's cells.

The reason some sea creatures such as Dolphins and whales need to surface in order to breath is due to the fact they are not amphibians like like fish but rather belong to the same animal group as humans meaning they are mammals.

Fact 20

Both land and water snails have eyes:

It is a common misconception that the tentacles that stick out of a snails head are its feelers however this is not the case.

Land snails have two sets of tentacles the larger ones are the ones that have the snails eyes attached. The positioning of the eyes is useful as this way they can move their tentacles around to get their desired view.

Water snails have only one pair of tentacles and their eyes are situated at the base of these which does not allow as much freedom of movement as that of a land snail.

Fact 21

Jimi Hendrix played a right handed Fender Stratocaster:

 Music star Jimi Hendrix who was famously left handed played a right handed Fender Stratocaster guitar upside down which just gives more credence to the guitar playing talent he undoubtedly had.

 Jimi Hendrix was born Johnny Allen Hendrix but after his father came back from fighting in world war two to discover that his wife had sent The future star to live with relatives after she was suffering from alcoholism. The war hero divorced his wife went and got his son back and renamed him James Marshall Hendrix.

Fact 22

The Taiga is the largest continuous biome in the world:

The Taiga biome is the largest terrestrial biome and extends across Europe, North America, and Asia. It is located right below the tundra biome The Taiga biome is also known as coniferous forest or boreal forest.

This biome typically has short, wet summers and long, cold winters. The Taiga gets plenty of snow during the winter months and its summer months sees plenty of rain fall.

Fires are common place in the Taiga biome . They are necessary for ridding the area of sick trees.

There are many countries located at least partly in the Taiga biome including: Russia, Norway,,Canada, Iceland, Finland, Sweden, Mongolia, Poland and the USA .

Fact 23

The term "Horsepower" was adopted in the late 18th century by Scottish engineer James Watt:

He used the term "Horsepower" to compare the output of steam engines with the strength of draft horses. It was later expanded to include things such as piston engines and electric motors. Horsepower is the measurement of power and the rate that work is done.

The mechanical horsepower which is also known as an imperial horsepower is 550 foot-pounds per second which is equivalent to 745,7 Watts

Fact 24

The gestation period of a human is 266 days:

The gestation of a human is 266 days, But what determines the length of an animals gestation period? The main factors seem to be an animals size and species, for example elephants two main species African and Asian) have different gestation periods. The gestation period of African elephants is 640 days, while the Asian elephant is 645 days.

For humans scientists discovered through the gestation period that it has evolutionary value in most societies it has always been men doing the hunting and women the gathering. Scientists discovered this was because the strains that hunting put on a woman doing 30 miles per day stopped a woman's period and thus were unable to ovulate this was discovered thanks to women who run marathons. This suggests the reason why the hunter gathering societies that survived were those with the women gathering and men hunting.

Fact 25

The last emperor of the Western Roman Empire was deposed by a German barbarian:

The Western Roman Empires last emperor was named Romulus Augustus. He was deposed by a German barbarian named Odoacer.

Odoacer was a mercenary leader in the Roman Imperial army he led a rebellion against the young emperor Romulus Augustus and proclaimed himself to be the king of Italy.

The Roman Empire did continue in the east but the crowning of Odoacer signalled the fall of the original Roman Empire.

Fact 26

The Epcot Centre opened on the 1st October 1982:

The Epcot Centre which was the second of four theme parks at Walt Disney world in Florida was opened on the 1st October 1982. The Epcot Centre covers around 300 acres of land and is twice the size of the Magic Kingdom land.

The Epcot Centre is dedicated to the celebration of human achievement such as technological innovation and international culture.

Fact 27

The worlds first computer was called ENIAC:

The worlds first computer was called ENIAC which stands for Electronic Numerical Integrator And Computer.

ENIAC was the first electronic general purpose computer and was capable of being reprogrammed to solve a large class of numerical problems.

The design and construction of ENIAC eas financed by the US army and the main purpose for it's invention was to calculate artillery firing tables for the army's ballistic research laboratory.

Fact 28

A moment is actually a medieval measurement of time which is equivalent to 1 minute 30 seconds:

The reasoning behind a moment being a measurement of time comes from the work of Bartholomeus Anglicus, who in 1240 wrote about each one hour segment of time is divided in to four points logically with one hour being 60 minutes this is the 15 minutes that make up a quarter of an hour.

But he writes each of these four sections are sub divided into a further ten segments which he calls moments lasting 1 minute 30 seconds each.

He goes further still saying each moment is divided into twelve ounces using the same mathematical rules that would add up to an ounce accounting for 7.5 seconds and each ounce into forty-seven atoms which is approximate 0.15 seconds.

<u>Fact 29</u>

Heineken International was founded in 1864 by Gerard Adriaan Heineken:

Heineken lager is a Dutch lager that is brewed in Amsterdam It was founded in 1864 by Gerard Adriaan Heineken

It was thanks to his mother buying De Hoolberg brewery for Gerard that he was able to embark on his successful brewing adventure

After Prohibition was lifted in 1933 Heineken was the first European beer to be imported to the United States.

Fact 30

Elvis Presley had a twin brother:

Elvis Aaron Presley was born in East Tupelo,Mississippi, on the 8th January 1935. He was a twin but unfortunately his brother who was named Jessie Garon was still born.

When Elvis was 13 he and his parents moved to Memphis where he attended Humes High-school.

Fact 31

Depending on a swans surroundings their average life span can range between 12-30 years:

If a swan lives with all the natural hazards that the wild has to offer such as vandals, pollution, overhead cables and pylons as-well as many other dangers then they have an average life expectancy of 12 years.

However for swans that live in a protected environment were they are well cared for will see their life expectancy rise dramatically to an average of 30 years.

<u>Fact 32</u>

At night-time some sea vessels have different coloured lights to indicate port side and starboard.

When standing on the Bridge of a ship and facing the the Bow which is the front of the ship Port refers to the left-hand side of the vessel whereas Starboard refers to the right-hand side of the vessel.

At night most sea vessels use a red navigation light to indicate Port side and a green navigation light to indicate Starboard.

Fact 33

The Louvre has 70,000 pieces of art:

Located in Paris, France The Louvre art museum. Is one of the the biggest of it's kind it holds 70,000 pieces of art which are spread over it's 650,000 square feet of gallery space. It is so big that it takes around 2,000 employees to maintain it..

The Louvre museum is housed in the Louvre palace on the 14th October 1750 King Louis XV sanctioned the first art display in the Louvre that consisted of 96 works of art from the royal collection.

Fact 34

Franklin D Roosevelt's wife Eleanor was the niece of another former president:

Some people believe that because Franklin D Roosevelt and Teddy Roosevelt share last names that they are very closely believing and has even been believed by some that they are father and son. However they are very distantly related so much so as being fifth cousins which is hardly a relation at all. However they do have a close tie that being that Franklin D Roosevelt married Eleanor who is the niece of Teddy Roosevelt

__Fact 35__

One oil barrel can hold 42 gallons of crude oil:

One oil barrel contains 42 gallons of crude oil which cam create around 45 gallons of finished product..For example in the USA one barrel of crude oil is used to make 19 gallons of gasoline, 12 gallons of diesel fuel, 4 gallons of jet fuel and 2 gallons of liquefied petroleum gas..

The largest oil reserve in the world is located in Venezuela which has around 298.35 million barrels.

Petrochemical found in oil helped to produce electrical devices such as computers.

Fact 36

The Heisman Memorial Trophy Award was created as a tribute to John Heisman:

Also known as The Heisman Trophy, The Heisman Memorial Trophy Award was created in memory of John Heisman and is awarded to annually to the most outstanding college football player.

It was created o in1935 by Down-town Athletic club after the death of John Heisman who was the clubs athletic director. Originally it was only awarded to the most valuable player in the east of the Mississippi but was expanded to include players west of the Mississippi.

Fact 37

The average colour of the Universe is beige:

Even though when we see the universe it just looks like a vast expansion of darkness with the odd light source of a blue star piercing through, scientists have determined that the Universe is actually a boring beige colour.

Another interesting find related to colour that research has found, is that the colour of stars are changing. Usually a cosmic blue colour stars in the Milky Way have been invaded by red coloured stars the change in colour is believed to be related to a stars temperature.

Fact 38

The first city to reach a population of 1 million:

Rome in Italy was the first city to reach a population of 1 million, they achieved this milestone in 133 B.C.

Here is a list of the first 10 cities that reached this milestone::

1- Rome.Italy. Achieved a population of 1 million in 133 B.C

2- Alexandria, Egypt. Achieved a population of 1 million in 30 B.C

3- Angkor, Cambodia. Achieved a population of 1 million in 900 A.D

4- Hangzhou, China. Achieved a population of 1 million in 1200 A.D

5- London,England. Achieved a population of 1 million in 1810 A.D

6- Paris,France. Achieved a population of 1 million in 1850 A.D

7- Beijing, China. Achieved a population of 1 million in 1855 A.D

8- Guangzhou,China. Achieved a population of 1 million in 1860 A.D

9- Berlin, Germany. Achieved a population of 1 million in 1870 A.D

10-Manhattan, USA. Achieved a population of 1 million in 1874 A.D

Fact 39

Australia first got it's own official currency in 1910:

Australia originally used the pound sterling same as the UK up until they got their own unique currency in 1910 which was called the Australian pound. Owing to devaluation of the Australian pound in 1931, the Australian government began to formulate a plan to change the currency and in 1966 the Australian pound was replaced by the Australian dollar. It is this currency that is still used today.

The Australian dollar was almost called the Australian Royal which was the name first agreed upon but the naming was put to a rethink at the last minute and the dollar was chosen.

Fact 40

The lines of latitude start at the equator:

The lines of latitude start at the equator and are measured at 90 degree angles. They measure north all the way to the North Pole and south all the way to the South Pole.

Each single degree of the total 180 degrees represents 60 Nautical miles on the surface of the Earth.

The lines of longitude also run north and south these lines are not parallel to each other.

Fact 41

The scale used to measure the resistance to scratching of a mineral is called a Mohs scale:

The Mohs scale is used to measure how hard or soft a mineral is by measuring the minerals resistance to scratching. There are 10 minerals on the Mohs scale that are ranked from softest up to hardest they are:

1- Talc

2- Gypsum

3- Calcite

4- Fluorite

5- Apatite

6- Orthoclase

7- Quartz

8- Topaz

9- Corundum

10- Diamond

Judging by the chart it can be determined that the softest mineral is talc meaning it is not very resistant whereas the most durable ranked hardest on the scale is diamond.

The Mohs scale was introduced between 1875-1880 and was named after a German mineralogist called Friedrich Mohs.

Fact 42

Alcohol is any drink that contains between 3-40% Ethanol:

Ethanol often called alcohol is a depressant psychoactive drug that in small doses can cause anxiety levels to drop and give you a high. However in large doses it can lead to being left in a drunken stupor and unconsciousness. It can also cause a physical dependence on the drug which is referred to as alcoholism.

Alcohol is separated into 3 main groups Wines, Beers and Spirits.

Fact 43

Penguins have special glands that can extract excess salt from the bloodstream which allows them to drink salt water.

When penguins are on land they will often find freshwaters to drink out of such as puddles and streams. They have also been known to drink rain water as it drops off them.

However when out at sea penguins are forced to drink salt water, luckily they have they have special glands located near the eye sockets the function of these glands is to remove excess salt from the blood stream meaning that for penguins it is relatively safe to drink the salt water.

Fact 44

The pledge of allegiance was written by Francis Bellamy:

Francis Bellamy wrote the pledge of allegiance in 1892. His original plan was to have all countries use the pledge of allegiance to their own countries Flag but was later adapted to become the American pledge of allegiance with a few changes in between. Here are some of the various versions with the changes underlined:

1892 first draft version- " I pledge allegiance to my Flag and the Republic for which it stands, one nation indivisible With liberty and justice for all"

1892-1923- "I pledge allegiance to my Flag and to the Republic for which it stands, one nation indivisible, with liberty and justice for all"

1923-1954- "I pledge allegiance to the Flag of the United States of America and to the Republic for which it stands, one nation indivisible, with liberty and justice for all"

1954(today's version)- "I pledge allegiance to the Flag of the United States of America, and to the Republic for which it stands,one Nation _under God_ indivisible, with liberty and justice for all."

They were the versions of Francis Bellamy and were originally based on a work composed in 1887 by Colonel George Bach.

George Bach's version went as follows:

" We give our heads and our hearts to God and or country. One language, one flag"

The pledge was not formerly adopted in to congress until 1942 and the official name " The Pledge of allegiance" was adopted in 1945.

The last words "under God" were added on Flag Day in 1954.

Fact 45

You have to be at least 35yrs old to be President of the USA:

Article 2 of the American constitution states the qualifications for becoming a president. To qualify to run for office a candidate must be 35 years or older, The candidate must also be a natural born citizen of the United States.

The longest serving president was Franklin D Roosevelt who was elected for 4 terms but died during his final term. By contrast the president who served the shortest time was William Henry Harrison he won the election by a landside unfortunately he died 32 days later.

One presidential term lasts for 4 years.

Fact 46

The band Lynyrd Skynyrd got their name from their school basketball coach:

Lynyrd Skynyrd took their name from their school basketball team coach whose name was Leonard Skinner after he told them their hair was to long.

The band popularized the Southern Rock Genre and are probably best known for the song "Sweet home Alabama" and "Freebird"

Unfortunately their was a tragic ending to the original band line-up when 3 of it's members died in a plane crash.

Fact 47

Tom Hanks plays Walt Disney in the film "Saving Mr Banks":

In the film "Saving Mr Banks" Tom Hanks played the part of Walt Disney. The film is based on a real event in Walt Disney's life.

When his daughters were young they loved a series of books based on a magical nanny named Mary Poppins. Walt Disney promises his daughters that someday he will make a film out of the series of books and 20 years later he delivered. But it was a painstaking endeavour. It took Walt Disney himself 16 years of trying to convince P.L Travers to let him make the film about Mary Poppins. She feared that Disney would make the main character a rosy cheeked delight when in the books she was slightly sadistic and she was right.

In reality Disney gave Travers script approval rights which Travers agreed to however their were arguments almost every step of the way but they finally agreed on a script. When filming Travers asked "When do we start cutting it?" But Disney told Travers "We don;t you have script approval rights not film editing rights" Which infuriated Travers.

She hated what Disney had done and swore that while she was alive Disney would never have the opportunity to defile her beloved Mary Poppins again. She even have it wrote in to her will stating specifically that if a stage musical was to be made hen the Sherman Brothers could not have anything to do with it and only English born writers could be used no Americans and absolutely nobody from the original film project could be involved.

<u>Fact 48</u>

Greece has 3 seas surrounding it:

Greece located in Southern Europe is located in the Southern end of the Balkan Peninsula, To the north Greece has Bulgaria, the Republic of Macedonia and Albania.

To the East Greece has both Turkey and the Aegean Sea.

To the West Greece has the Ionian Sea

While to the South lies the Mediterranean Sea

Fact 49

Isaac Newton composed the visible Colour Spectrum:

Isaac Newton composed the visible colour spectrum. This is the electromagnetic spectrum that is visible to the human eye. The spectrum consists of 7 colours being Red, Orange, Yellow, Green, Blue, Indigo and Violet.

The spectrum does however miss out some colours that the human eye can see such as pink and purple

Isaac Newton is also the founder of the laws of gravity he discovered the laws when sitting under a tree and an apple fell upon his head.

Fact 50

Balsa wood is one of the lightest least dense wood there is:

Balsa wood is considered a hardwood, it is one of the lightest woods around.

The way to make the distinction between a hardwood and softwood has a lot to do with the reproduction process of the plant it comes from. The seeds of the different trees vary in their structure.

Hardwood trees are angiosperms. This means they produce seeds with some sort of covering such as fruit or a hard covering like an acorn.

Softwoods are gymnosperms. This means that these trees just let the seeds fall to the ground as they are Pine trees fall into this category.

Fact 51

Contrary to popular belief Baseball was not invented by Abner Doubleday:

Many people believe that before he went on to be a Civil War hero a young man named Abner Doubleday invented Baseball in 1839 in Cooperstown, New York. This however is not possible as Doubleday was still in West Point ij 1839 not only that but Abner Doubleday never once claimed to have anything to do with Baseball.

The real origin of Baseball is a little more complicated as a sport resembling Baseball in the USA date back to the 1700s. Baseball itself seems to be the offspring of two games from England them being Rounders and Cricket.

In 1845 a group of men from New York City founded The New York Knickerbocker Baseball Club. One member Alexander Joy Cartwright who as-well as being a bank clerk was also a volunteer firefighter provided new rules that form the basis of the Baseball we know today.

Fact 52

Thunder is actually just the sound that Lightening makes:

Thunder is a sound caused by lightening the sound of the thunder depends on the distance and type of lightening it can range from a loud sharp bang to a long low rumble.

Thunder is caused by the sudden increase in pressure and temperature caused by the lightening producing rapid expansion of the air surrounding and within a bolt of lightening. The expansion of air then creates a sonic shock wave similar to a sonic boom which is the thunder.

Fact 53

The first SMS messages known as Text messages was sent in 1992:

The concept of the SMS service was developed in the Franco-German GSM company in 1984 by Friedhelm Hillebrand and Bernard Ghillebaert.

The first text message was sent in 1992 by Neil Papworth who was a former developer at Sema Group Company it simply said "Merry Christmas" and it was sent to and successfully received by Richard Jarvis of Vodafone.

Fact 54

Pizza Hut was first created by the Carney brothers in 1958:

It all started for Dan and Frank Carney when their mother gave them a loan of $600 which in 1958they used to open the worlds first Pizza Hut. It was located in Wichita USA. As I am sure you have guessed it was a monumental success for the brothers.

They opened the first Pizza Hut in the UK in 1973 and is one of if not the biggest name in the pizza industry.

Fact 55

Bats are the only mammals that can fly:

Bats are the only mammals that can truly fly. Some may argue that the flying squirrel also flies but the fact is that the flying squirrel can only glide over short distances, similar to the gliding opposum.

Bats are not totally blind they have very poor eye sight however and are able to fly by listening to and feeling the sound vibrations that bounce off each object.

Fact 56

Rum is made from Sugar-cane by-products:

Rum is a distilled alcoholic beverage made from Sugar-cane by-products, such as molasses, or directly from Sugar cane juice, by a process of fermentation and distillation. The distillate, a clear liquid, is then usually aged in oak barrels.

Predecessors to the Rum of today is thought to date back thousands of years. There was one such drink named Brum. Marco Polo also recorded an account of "a very good wine of sugar" that was offered to him in what is now modern day Iran.

Fact 57

The white wedding dress was made popular by Queen Victoria:

The white wedding dress was not always the default colour when a lady was getting married in western culture. It was made popular by Queen Victoria at her wedding to Prince Albert in 1840. nor does it symbolize what virginity or purity as is believed.

It is considered rebellious by some to wear any other colour garment than white when getting married but for centuries that was actually the norm.

The colour white was actually a symbol of wealth with clothes being a painstaking exercise to wash it was considered a symbol of wealth to buy a sparkling white garment that was only ever going to be worn once.

__Fact 58__

__Daddy long legs (spiders) do not carry the most potent venom.__

The most poisonous spiders in the world are the Pholcids Daddy long legs even more so than any Funnel web or Black widow spider surely this can not be true?....well it is not

It is a common misconception that even though they carry a poison that, A) It is the most poisonous spider in the world. And,B) they have no way of administering it to damage any person. However neither of these statements are true the structure of a Daddy long legs fangs is similar to the dynamics of most brown recluse spiders. This means that they are theoretically capable of breaking a person's skin, luckily however they have no natural inclination to bite people.

And while they do have poison, to say that it is the most potent amongst the spiders is quite an over exaggeration. As was proved by the team at "Mythbusters".

Fact 59

Rubies and Sapphires are the same mineral just different colours:

Rubies and Sapphires are the same minerals just different colours. They are both gems produced by Corundum. Ruby is the red variety while Sapphires encompass all the other colours.

It is possible to enhance the colours of Rubies and Sapphires by applying a heat treatment to them.

Fact 60

A horse generally has 205 bones:

 The skeleton of a horse is made up of 205 bones they consist of: 54 making up the vertebral column, 36 rib bones, 1 sternum, 40 bones in the front legs, 40 in the hind legs and 34 in the skull.

 The height of a horse is measured in a unit known as hands each one hand accounts for 4 inches.

Fact 61

Killer whales are actually members of the dolphin family:

Killer whales also known as orcas are the biggest members of the dolphin family. Even though they are members of the dolphin family who are generally considered to be friendly gentle animals, Orcas are one of the worlds most powerful predators.

Orcas tend to hunt in families of up to 40 members and they work as a team to hunt and catch their chosen prey.

Fact 62

The popular treat M&M's were first introduced by Mars Incorporated in 1941:

The treats known as M&M's which are produced by Mars Incorporated was first introduced in the USA in 1941 and are now sold in around 100 countries worldwide.

It is estimated that on any given day over 400 million individual M&M's are produced in the USA.

It is believed the hard Candy coated shell of the chocolate was originally inspired by a method used to allow soldiers to carry chocolate without it melting. This is reflected by the companies longest lasting slogan "Melts in your mouth, not in your hand"

Fact 63

In 2012 London became the first city to host the Modern day Olympics three times:

London, England, held the summer Olympics in 2012, in doing so it became the first city ever to host the games for a third time.

The years that London held the Olympic games are: 1908, 1948 and 2012

The 1908 Olympics was originally scheduled to be held in Rome however the eruption of Mount Vesuvius meant the games were relocated to London

The 1948 Olympics was the first Post WW II Olympic Games.

Fact 64

The cracking sound that a whip makes when properly wielded is actually a small sonic boom:

When a whip is used for whatever reason such as you see in films or as have been used on people and animals for various reasons the cracking sound you hear when the whip is struck is actually a small sonic boom.

This is caused because the end of the whip known as the "cracker" moves faster than the speed of sound

It is believed that the whip is possibly the first human invention to break the speed barrier.

Fact 65

Ginger ale can be good for soothing coughs and/or nausea:

Ginger products such as Ginger Ale has been found to help with ailments such as coughs, sore throats and nausea.

Thomas Cantrell, an American apothecary and surgeon, claimed to have invented ginger ale in Belfast, Northern Ireland, and marketed it with local beverage manufacturer Grattan and Company. Grattan embossed the slogan "The Original Makers of Ginger Ale" on its bottles.

Fact 66

The reason you say "Roger that" over a radio is because in the R used to be Roger and was used instead of received:

The reason "Roger that" is said over a radio is because R is for "received and understood"in radio protocol , in the old Phonetic alphabet R used to be Roger however that has now changed to Romeo but Roger is still used to mean received over radio transmissions.

In the RAF they say "Roger Willco" which means "Received will co-operate"

Fact 67

The duck-billed platypus is native to Eastern Australia:

The duck-billed platypus is a semi-aquatic egg laying mammal. It is native to Eastern Australia so is found in places such as Tasmania.

The platypus is one of only five species of mammals that lay eggs the other four are all species of echidna.

Fact 68

Dr Seuss wrote a book with only 50 different words in it:

 Popular children's author Dr Seuss was challenged by the founder of the publishing firm that he could not write an entertaining children's book using only 50 different words. Dr Seuss took on the challenge and a wager of $50 was placed between the 2 men. The resulting book was "Green eggs and ham" and it went on to become one of Dr Seuss most popular works, selling over 200 million copies. I think it safe to say Dr Seuss comfortably won that bet.

 Dr Seuss real name is Theo Geisel and through this book he learned that setting constraints on himself woke his creative side and he used the same method only changing it slightly for future books, for example using only first grade vocabulary in his hit book "The cat in the hat".

Fact 69

Grover Cleveland featured on the $1,000 bill:

The USA at one time issued bills as big as $10,000 dollars until 1969 when the treasury announced that the bigger bills were going out of circulation (they are still legal to spend today though if you are lucky enough to own one)

There was even a $2 bill that seems to be rarely seen.

53 People have appeared on US bank notes of various types they are

John Quincy Adams $500 (1869)

Thomas Hart Benton $100 (1870)

Salmon Portland Chase $1 (1862),$10 (1863-64), $1,000 (1861), $10,000 (1918), $10,000 (1928-1934)

William Clark $10 (1901)

Henry Clay- $50 (1869)

Grover Cleveland- $20 (1914-15), $1,000 (1928-1934)

DeWitt Clinton- $1,000 (1869)

Stephen Decatur- $20 (1878)

Edward Everett- $50 (1878)

David Glasgow Farragut- $100 (1890)

William Pitt Fessenden- $20 (1882)

Benjamin Franklin- $50 (1974), $10 (1979), $100 (1914), $100 (1928-present)

Robert Fulton- $2 (1896)

Albert Gallatin- $500 (1862)

James Abram Garfield $5 (1882), $20 (1882)

Ulusses Simpson Grant- $1 (1899), $5 (1886 and 1896), $50 (1913-14, 1918 and 1928-present)

Alexander Hamilton-$5 (1861), $2 (1862), $5 (1862), $20 (1869), $50 (1862), $50 (1863), $50 (1864), $500 (1864), $1,000 (1918), $1,000 (1870), $10 (1928-present)

Winfield Scott Hancock- $2 (1886)

Benjamin Harrison- $5 (1902)

Thomas Andrews Hendricks- $10 (1886)

Michael Hillegas- $10 (1907)

Andrew Jackson- $5 (1869), $10,000 (1878), $50 (1861), $10 (1915), $10 (1914), $10,000 (1870), $20 (1928-present)

Thomas Jefferson- $2 (1869), $2 (1918), $2 (1928-present)

John Jay Knox Jr- $100 (1902)

Meriwether Lewis- $10 (1901)

Abraham Lincoln-$1 (1861), $10 (1862), $100 (1869), $20 (1864), $1 (1899), $5 (1923), $5 (1914-15), $500 (1870) $5 (1928-present)

James Madison-$5,000 (1878), $5,000 (1918), $5,000 (1870), $5,000 (1928-1934)

Daniel Manning- $20 (1886)

Joseph King Fenno Mansfield- $500 (1874)

William Leonard Marcy- $1,000 (1878)

John Marshall- $20 (1890), $500 (1918)

Hugh McCulloch- $20 (1902)

William McKinley Jr- $10 (1902), $500 (1928-1934)

James Birdseye McPherson- $2 (1890)

George Gordon Meade- $1,000 (1890)

James Monroe- $100 (1878)

Robert Morris- $1,000 (1862), $10 (1878)

Samuel Finley Breese Morse- $2 (1896)

Running Antelope- $5(1899)

Winfield Scott- $500 (1861), $100 (1864)

William Henry Seward- $50 (1891)

Phillip Henry Sheridan- $5 (1896), $10 (1890)

John Sherman-$50 (1902)

William Tecumseh Sherman- $500 (1891)

Edward McMasters Stanton- $1 (1890)

Charles Sumner- $500 (1878)

George H Thomas- $5 (1890)

George Washington- $1 (1869), $100 (1863), $100 (1864), $1,000 (1861), $500 (1861) $1 (1896), $1 (1923), $2 (1899), $1 (1918), $20 (1905), $1 (1928-present)

Martha Washington- $1 (1886), $1 (1896)

Daniel Webster- $10 (1869)

Woodrow Wilson- $100,000 (1934)

William Windom-$2 (1891)

Silas Wright Jr- $50 (1882)

Fact 70

The bird that migrates the furthest is the arctic tern:

When migrating the bird that holds the record for the longest distance travelled is the arctic tern this bird native to areas around the Arctic and sub-Arctic as the name would suggest this sea bird makes a trip of 44,000 miles every year.

The arctic tern sometimes called the sea swallow has the appearance of a white face with a black cap.

The scientific name for the arctic tern is Sterna paradisaea.

Fact 71

On average sea level is about 20cm higher on the Pacific side than on the Atlantic:

The average sea level is 20cm higher on the Pacific side than on the Atlantic side. This is due to the water being less dense on the Pacific side, due to prevailing weather and ocean conditions. These differences in sea level are common across many short sections of land that divide ocean basins.

The Pacific ocean is the largest of the oceans and it covers around 30% of the worlds surface. The original meaning of the name Pacific ocean was Peaceful sea.

Fact 72

Dutch settlers in South Africa were survivors of a shipwreck:

The first Dutch settlement in South Africa was in March 1647, They arrived on the Dutch ship Nieuwe Haarlem which met with an accident at the Cape.

The survivors of the resulting shipwreck built a small fort which they named "Sand Fort of the Cape of Good Hope"

after almost a year they were rescued by a fleet of 12 ships under the command of W.G De Jong.

Fact 73

The first expedition around the world was led by Ferdinand Magellen:

Ferdinand Magellan was a Portuguese explorer who lead the first ever expedition to sail around the world. The voyage started for Ferdinand in 1519 and ended in 1522.

The start of the voyage was Seville in Spain a group of 5 ships left on the voyage they were: The Trinidad, San Antonio, Conception, Victoria and Santiago. Only one ship completed the voyage back to Seville that was Victoria.

Ferdinand Magellan the man responsible for naming the Pacific ocean unfortunately never completed the journey as he was unfortunately killed near the end of the trip during a battle with the natives of the Island of Mactan in the Phillippines. The rest of the journey was led by navigator Juan Sebastian Elcano. Out of the original 270 crew members n board only 18 returned alive.

Fact 74

The Sony companies first ever product was an electrical rice cooker:

After losing the war in 1945 Sony founder Masaru ibuka noticed there were millions of homes which had an electrotype supply but lacked the appliances to make it worth while and set about inventing and producing the electric rice cooker.

The product was a disaster and hardly ever worked as intended.

Before Sony became an Incorporated company it ran under the name including during the time the rice cooker was released in 1945 of "Tokyo Telecommunications engineering corporation.

Fact 75

There are countries were a nod of the head means no:

In most countries around the world nodding your head generally is a sign of yes or positive answer, whereas shaking the head is generally taken to be a sign of saying no or a negative answer.

There are countries however where the opposite is true these countries include Greece, Albania, Bulgaria and Macedonia.

There is also an unknown disease that usually affects children under 15 called nodding syndrome.

Fact 76

The chief author of the Declaration of Independence was Thomas Jefferson:

The Declaration of Independence was a document that was signed by a group of men representing all the colonies of the USA at the time. The chief author was Thomas Jefferson who it is believed was given the task by his good friend John Adams. The Declaration pledges the colonies lives,fortunes and Sacred honour to each other. It is possibly the most important document in American history.

There are 56 people to sign the document they are as follows:

Samuel Huntington (Connecticut)

Roger Sherman (Connecticut)

William Williams (Connecticut)

Oliver Wolcott (Connecticut)

Thomas McKean (Delaware)

George Read (Delaware)

Caesar Rodney (Delaware)

Button Gwinnett (Georgia)

Lyman Hall (Georgia)

George Walton (Georgia)

Charles Carroll (Maryland)

Samuel Chase (Maryland)

William Paca (Maryland)

Thomas Stone (Maryland)

John Adams (Massachusetts)

Samuel Adams (Massachusetts)

Elbridge Gerry (Massachusetts)

John Hancock (Massachusetts)

Robert Treat Paine (Massachusetts)

Josiah Bartlett (New Hampshire)

Matthew Thornton (New Hampshire)

William Whipple (New Hampshire)

Abraham Clark (New Jersey)

John Hart (New Jersey)

Francis Hopkinson (New Jersey)

Richard Stockton (New Jersey)

John Witherspoon (New Jersey)

William Floyd (New York)

Francis Lewis (New York)

Philip Livingston (New York)

Lewis Morris (New York)

Joseph Hewes (North Carolina)

William Hooper (North Carolina)

John Penn (North Carolina)

George Clymer (Pennsylvania)

Benjamin Franklin (Pennsylvania)

Robert Morris (Pennsylvania)

John Morton (Pennsylvania)

George Ross (Pennsylvania)

Benjamin Rush (Pennsylvania)

James Smith (Pennsylvania)

George Taylor (Pennsylvania)

James Wilson (Pennsylvania)

Thomas Heywood Jr (South Carolina)

Thomas Lynch Jr (South Carolina)

Arthur Middleton (South Carolina)

Edward Routledge (South Carolina)

William Ellery (Rhode Island)

Stephen Hopkins (Rhode Island)

Carter Braxton (Virginia)

Benjamin Harrison (Virginia)

Thomas Jefferson (Virginia)

Francis Lightfoot Lee (Virginia)

Richard Henry Lee (Virginia)

Thomas Nelson Jr (Virginia)

George Wythe (Virginia)

Fact 77

A Nile Crocodile can hold it's breath for up to 2 hours:

A Nile crocodile will dive underwater for only a few minutes unless they feel they are under threat, in which case they will stay under water for up to 30 minutes. If a Nile crocodile remains in an inactive state it can hold it's breath for up to 2 hours.

An average adult male crocodile can grow as big as 16 ft 5inches however there has been specimens recorded as big as 20ft in length.

Fact 78

Buckingham Palace has 775 rooms:

Buckingham Palace has 775 rooms. These include 19 State rooms, 52 Royal and guest bedrooms, 188 staff bedrooms, 92 offices and 78 bathrooms.

Buckingham Palace is the home of the British Monarchy, Which at the time of writing this is Queen Elizabeth II and her family.

Fact 79

The first Spaniard to set foot on what is now the United States was Juan Ponce De Leon:

When Juan Ponce De/Leon sailed with Christopher Columbus to what is now the United States, he became the first Spaniard to ever set foot on that land.

Juan Ponce De Leon was also the first ever Governor of Puerto Rico after being appointed to the position by the Spanish crown.

Fact 80

Jury nullification is when a jury acquits someone even if they feel he/she is guilty:

When a jury acquits a defendant even though they believe them to be guilty it is called jury nullification.

This may occur when jury members disagree with each other, or if they believe the defendant did it but either !) do not believe they should be punished for it, or 2) Do not agree with the law the defendant is said to have broken.

Fact 81

Led Zeppelin had an album that was not given a title:

When English rock band Led Zeppelin made their fourth studio album they neglected to name it and so it is generally referred to as simply "Led Zeppelin IV"

Released in 1971 this album contains one of the bands most famous and best loved songs "Stairway to Heaven"

Fact 82

"Hello" was not always the universal way to answer a telephone it was originally "Ahoy":

"Hello used to be an expression of mild surprise as in "Hello what is this then?" or an old fashioned policeman's "Hello hello hello, what's all this then". This was still the case when Alexander Graham Bell created the telephone and he originally had it decided that the shipping term "Ahoy" would be the greeting when answering a telephone.

It is believed Thomas Edison was the first person to use the word "hello" as a greeting.

Fact 83

Egyptian Hieroglyphs is believed to be the worlds oldest form of writing:

According to experts Egyptian hieroglyphs may be the oldest form of writing. It is believed that the hieroglyphs date as far back as around 3,300 BC.

Ancient Egyptian hieroglyphs are comprised of between 700-800 different basic symbols called glyphs however as the years passed this number grew.

Fact 84

Geoffrey Chaucer printed the first apple pie recipe:

Apple pie was invented in Europe at some point during the 14th century. Within this same century the first apple pie recipe was put in to print in 1381 by renowned poet and author Geoffrey Chaucer.

Known as the father of English literature Geoffrey Chaucer's most famous work is possibly The Canterbury Tales. Filled with a mixture of stories set as a group of people telling each-other tales as they travel from London to Canterbury to visit the shrine of Thomas Becket. As far as books go it is a masterpiece and on a personal note would be highly recommended to any lover of books.

Fact 85

Kiribati is the only country in the world that is situated in all 4 hemispheres:

Kiribati which is located in the central Pacific ocean is an Island nation that comprises of 33 atolls and reef islands aswell as a raised coral island named Banaba. It is the only country to be situated in the Northern, Southern, Eastern and Western hemispheres.

Kiribati uses the Australian Dollar as it's currency. The capital of Kiribati is Tarawa

Fact 86

The first African-American to win an Academy Award was Hattie McDaniel:

Hattie McDaniel became the first African-American to win an Academy Award. She won the best supporting actress award in 1939 for her role as "Mammy" in "Gone with the wind"

Hattie McDaniel was a very talented lady and aswell as being an actress she was also a professional singer and was the first black woman to sing on the radio in the United States.

Fact 87

Devils Tower was the first US national monument:

On the 24th September 1906 President Theodore Roosevelt established the first US national monument it was located in Wyoming and called Devils Tower.

There are 122 national monuments in the US they are:

Admirality Island (Alaska) (Est.1978)

African Burial Ground (New York) (Est. 2006)

Agate Fossil Beds (Nebraska) (Est.1997)

Agus Fria (Arizona) (Est.2000)

Alibates Flint Quarries (Texas) (Est. 1965)

Aniakchak (Alaska) (Est. 1978)

Aztec Ruins (New Mexico) (Est. 1923)

Bandeiler (New Mexico) (Est. 1916)

Basin an Range (Nevada (Est. 2015)

Belmont-Paul Women's Equality (District of Columbia) (Est. 2016)

Berryessa Snow Mountain (California) (Est. 2015)

Booker-T Washington (Virginia) (Est. 1956)

Browns Canyon (Colorado) (Est. 2015)

Buck Island Reef (US Virgin Islands) (Est. 1961)

Cabrillo (California) (Est. 1913)

California Coastal (California) (Est. 2000)

Canyon De Chelly (Arizona) (Est. 1931)

Canyons of the Ancients (Colorado) (Est. 2000)

Cape Krusenstern (Alaska) (Est. 1978)

Capulin Volcano (New Mexico) (Est. 1916)

Carrizo Plain (California) (Est. 2001)

Casa Grande Ruins (Arizona) (Est. 1918)

Cascade Siskiyou (Oregon) (Est. 2000)

Castillo de San Marcos (Florida) (Est. 1924)

Castle Clinton (New York) (Est. 1946)

Castle Mountains (California) (Est. 2016)

Cedar Breaks (Utah) (Est. 1933)

Cesar E Chavez (California) (Est. 2012)

Charles Young Buffalo Soldiers (Ohio) (Est. 2013)

Chimney Rock (Colorado) (Est. 2012)

Chiicahua (Arizona) (Est. 1924)

Colorado (Colorado) (Est.1911)

Craters of the Moon (Idaho) (Est. 1924)

Devils Postpile (California) (Est. 1911)

Devils Tower (Wyoming) (Est. 1906)

Dinosaur (Colorado/Utah) (Est. 1915)

Effigy Mounds (Iowa) (Est. 1949)

El Malpais (New Mexico) (Est. 1987)

El Morro (New Mexico) (Est. 1906)

Florissant Fossil Beds (Colorado) (Est. 1969)

Fort Frederica (Georgia) (Est. 1936)

Fort Matanzas (Florida) (Est. 1924)

Fort McHenry (Maryland) (Est. 1925)

Fort Monroe (Virginia) (Est. 2011)

Fort Ord (California) (Est. 2012)

Fort Pulaski (Georgia) (Est. 1924)

Fort Stanwix (New York) (Est. 1935)

Fort Sumter (South Carolina) (Est. 1948)

Fort Union (New Mexico) (Est. 1956)

Fossil Butte (Wyoming) (Est. 1972)

George Washington Birthplace (Virginia) (Est. 1930)

George Washington Carver (Missouri) (Est. 1943)

Giant Sequoia (California) (Est. 2000)

Gila Cliff Dwellings (New Mexico) (Est. 1907)

Governors Island (New York) (Est. 2001)

Grand Canyon Parashant (Arizona) (Est. 2000)

Grand Portage (Minnesota) (Est. 1960)

Grand Staircase Escalante (Utah) (Est. 1996)

Hagerman Fossil Beds (Idaho) (Est. 1988)

Hanford Reach (Washington) (Est. 2000)

Harriet Tubman Underground Railroad (Maryland) (Est. 2013))

Hohokam Pima (Arizona) (Est. 1972)

Homestead (Nebraska) (Est. 1936)

Honouliuli (Hawaii) (Est. 2015)

Hovenweep (Colorado/Utah) (Est. 1923)

Ironwood Forest (Arizona) (Est. 2000)

Jewel Cave (South Dakota) (Est. 1908)

John Day Fossil Beds (Oregon) (Est. 1974)

Kasha Katuwe Tent Rocks (New Mexico) (Est. 2001)

Lava Beds (California) (Est. 1925)

Little Bighorn Battlefield (Montana (Est. 1940)

Marrianas Trench Marine (Northern Mariana, Guam) (Est. 2009)

Military Working Dog Teams (Texas) (Est. 2013)

Misty Fjords (Alaska) (Est. 1978)

Mojave Trails (California) (Est. 2016)

Montezuma Castle (Arizona) (Est. 1906)

Mount St Helens (Washington) (Est. 1982)

Muir Woods (California) (Est. 1908)

Natural Bridges (Utah) (Est. 1908)

Navajo (Arizona) (Est. 1909)

Newberry (Oregon) (Est. 1990)

Ocmulgee (Georgia) (Est. 1936)

Oregon Caves (Oregon) (Est.1909)

Organ Mountains Desert Peaks (New Mexico) (Est. 2014)

Pacific Remote Islands Marine (Hawaii,US Minor Outlying Islands) (Est. 2009)

Papahanaumokuakea Marine (Hawaii, US Minor Outlying Islands) (Est. 2006)

Petroglyph (New Mexico) (Est. 1990)

Pipe Spring (Arizona) (Est. 1923)

Pipestone (Minnesota) (Est. 1937)

Pompeys Pillar (Montana) (Est. 2001)

Poverty Point (Louisiana) (Est. 1988)

Prehhistoric Trackways (New Mexico)

President Lincoln's Cottage at the Soldiers' home (District of Columbia) (Est. 2000)

Pullman (Illinois) (Est. 2015)

Rainbow Bridge (Utah) (Est. 1910)

Rio Grande Del Norte (New Mexico) (Est. 2013)

Rose Atoll Marine (American Samoa) (Est. 2009)

Russel Cave (Alabama) (Est. 1961)

Salinas Pueblo Missions (New Mexico) (Est. 1909)

San Gabriel Mountains (California) (Est. 2014)

San Juan Islands (Washington) (Est. 2013)

Sand to Snow (California) (Est. 2016)

Santa Rosa and San Jacinto Mountains (California) (Est. 2000)

Scotts Bluff (Nebraska) (Est. 1919)

Sonoran Desert (Arizona) (Est. 2001)

Statue of Liberty (New York, New Jersey) (Est. 1924)

Stonewall (New York) (Est. 2016)

Sunset Crater (Arizona) (Est. 1930)

Timpanogos Cave (Utah) (Est. 1922)

Tonto (Arizona) (Est. 1907)

Tule Springs Fossil Beds (Nevada) (Est. 2014)

Tuzgoot (Arizona) (Est. 1939)

Upper Missouri River Breaks (Montana) (Est. 2001)

Vermilion Cliffs (Arizona) (Est. 2000)

Virgin Islands Coral Reef (US Virgin Islands) (Est. 2001)

Waco Mammoth (Texas) (Est. 2015)

Walnut Canyon (Arizona) (Est. 1915)

White Sands (New Mexico) (Est. 1933)

World War II Valor in the Pacific
(Hawaii,Alaska,California) (Est. 2008)

Wupatki (Arizona) (Est. 1924)

Yucca House (Colorado) (Est. 1919)

Fat 88

Ada Lovelace wrote the first computer program:

Ada Byron, who became Ada Countess of Lovelace, known simply as Ada Lovelace. Wrote the first computer program and was employed by Charles Babbage to translate his papers in to English for his Analytical Machine.

Ada Lovelace is the only legitimate child of poet George Lord Byron and wife Anna Isabella Milbanke "Annabella". While George Lord Byron had other children they were born out of wedlock to other women.

Fact 89

The liver is the only internal organ capable of regenerating itself:

The only internal organ in the human body that is capable of natural regeneration is the liver.

If you have as little as 25% of your liver given enough time it can regenerate in to a full liver. Regeneration is rapid and a removal of around 50% of the livers entire mass can see it fully regenerate within 2 weeks.

Fact 90

A mile takes the average person 2,000 steps to complete:

It takes the average person 2,000 steps to complete a mile walk which means every 10,000 steps you take is 5 miles worth of walking.

In time taken the average person walks around 3.5mph that averages out to around 17mins per mile.

Fact 91

Construction of The Washington DC Metro-rail system:

Construction of the Metro system in DC began on 9th December1969. The first stations on the line opened on 27th March 1976.

Consisting of 5 lines which contains 83 stations covering a distance of around 103 miles of track the original plan that was put in place for the Metro system was not fully completed until 13th January

Fact 92

Martin Van Buren was the first president to be born a citizen of the United States of America:

Martin Van Buren born on the 5th December 1782, was the first president to be born after the USA had gained independence so was officially the first president born as a citizen of the United States.

The first of the log cabin presidents (president born in a log cabin) was Andrew Jackson born on 15th March 1767

Jimmy Carter born 1st October 1924 was the first president to be born in a hospital.

Fact 93

Mark Twain took his name from a term used on river boats:

Famous author Mark Twain was born with the name Samuel Langhorne Clemens and used the pen name Mark Twain when he began writing. He got his name from a river boat term measuring 2 fathoms which is 12ft in depth. Mark(measure) Twain(two)

Mark Twain is the author of such classics as "The Adventures of Huckleberry Finn"

Fact 94

Oprah Winfrey was meant to be named Orpah:

The much loved American TV personality Oprah Winfrey was originally meant to be named Orpah but after her name was misspelled on her birth certificate it stated her name was Oprah and the name stuck.

Orpah who Oprah was supposed to be named after was the sister-in-law of Ruth in the bible.

Fact 95

Imitation crab meat is minced fish:

Imitation crab meat is made from de boning and mincing white fleshed fish such as Pollack or Whiting. The mince is then made in to a paste.

The practice of mincing the fish was developed in Japan around 1,000 years ago.

Fact 96

All mammals have 7 Cervical Vertebrae:

The cervical vertebrae are located in the neck area it is a common theme among mammals (humans included) that we have 7 of them in the neck.

The cervical vertebrae are the smallest of the true vertebrae.

Fact 97

Clown fish change their gender:

Clown fish such as that in the children's film "Finding Nemo" change there gender: A school of clown fish live within a hierarchy with a female at the top and when the female dies the most dominant male changes their gender and becomes the new female. So by the end of ""Finding Nemo" the title characters dad would have been his mother by the time he found him.

Other species of fish are known to change their gender such as: wrasses, moray eels and gobies.

Fact 98

When a person pays bail money they get it refunded:

When a person who is set to stand trial for whatever reason pays bail they are entitled to get it refunded if they show up for all of their court dates regardless if they are guilty or innocent. Should they fail to show up to any dates the court are entitled to keep it and the person who paid the bail will not get a penny back.

Fact 99

The first ever thanksgiving was in the August of 1623:

The first ever thanksgiving was in August 1621 when the 53 surviving pilgrims celebrated their successful harvest, as was the English custom. During this time, "many of the Indians coming amongst the rest their great king Massasoit, with some ninety men." That 1621 celebration is remembered as the "First Thanksgiving in Plymouth." However the Pilgrims did not call this feast a Thanksgiving feast the firs time they celebrated Thanksgiving was in 1623 to give thanks for the rainfall.

Fact 100

The knee joint is the largest in the human body:

The knee joint joins the thigh with the leg and consists of two articulations: one between the femur and tibia, and one between the femur and patella. It is the largest joint in the human body..

While it is the largest joint in the human body with many functions it is also vulnerable to injury.

Other Books By Jack Lexington

Non-Fiction

A worldwide Collection Of Unsolved Murders: Series 1 United Kingdom Book 1(1536-1969)

A worldwide Collection Of Unsolved Murders: Series 1 United Kingdom Book 2 (1970-1994

The A-Z of Random Facts

Past Civilizations, Tribes and Empires

Presidents of the USA: From Washington to Obama

Short Fiction

Dead as a Doornail

Childrens Books

The Adventures of Princess Lexi: Journey to the Wibbly Wobbly Mountain

Poetry Book

The Little chapbook of short and simple poems